The Honkbon

The slinx is plodding across the soft, orange sand.
He is still tracking down the grinlings.
The planet of Zaxon has a big red sun, so it gets very, very hot.
The slinx wishes he had something to drink.

Write
The slinx can still see the prints of the grinlings.
He wishes he had a _____.

At last the orange sand comes to an end.

Now the slinx has to cross a flat stretch of rock.

There are some big black cracks in this rock.

The slinx has to jump across some of these cracks.

It is a good job that he can jump well.

He must not drop down one of the cracks.

Draw the slinx jumping across one of the cracks.

Write

Now the slinx must cross a stretch of _ _ _ _.

There are some zig-zag cracks in the rock.

In the end the slinx sees some cliffs.
He can just see some little houses
on top of one of the cliffs.
The slinx sticks at it until he gets
to the bottom of this cliff.

The slinx goes scrambling up
the cliff.
There is a big rock at the top.
Will it drop down on him?

The slinx gets to the top and stands at the back of the big rock.
Now the slinx can see the houses.
They are plastic and glass houses.
There are lots of grinlings living in these houses.
Some of them are getting dinner ready in a big pot.
One of the grinlings rings a bell, then everyone grabs a dish and comes running up.
The grinlings love to eat.
The slinx licks his lips.
The dinner smells very good.

Draw the plastic and glass houses.

Write

The slinx can _ _ _ _ _ the dinner.

He _ _ _ _ _ his lips.

Then the slinx hiccups!
Everyone stops eating.
At first, the slinx thinks that they
are all going to run off.
But then they all rush at him.
They grab his hands and legs
and drag him across to the
big pot.
The slinx is in a panic.
He sees one of the grinlings lifting
up the lid.
He thinks that they are going to
eat him!

**Draw the grinling lifting the
lid off the pot.**
Write
The slinx _ _ _ _ _ _ _ and the
grinlings spot him.
They drag him across to the _ _ _ .

But then, one of the grinlings picks up a dish and fills it with dinner.

He passes it to the slinx.

Everyone grins.

The slinx sits down and tucks in.

He asks for some more.

It is astonishing because the grinlings understand every word.

The slinx eats some more and then they pull him across to one of the houses.

They give him a soft mattress to sleep on, and a thick rug for a blanket.

He stretches out and goes to sleep.

Write

The grinlings give the slinx some dinner and a _____ to sleep on.

The slinx sleeps very well.
Two of the grinlings bring him a
drink and something to eat.
Then he steps out of the house and
has a good stretch.
Then—

THUD! THUD! THUD!

Something very big is trampling
across the rock.

Write

The slinx comes out of the house
and has a _____.
Then there is a THUD.
Something ___ is coming.

15

The grinlings panic.
They yell out.

'The Honkbonk!'
'The Honkbonk is coming!'
'Run for it!'

And they rush across to the houses.
In less than ten seconds, they are
all well hidden.
The slinx is just left standing there!

Draw the grinlings running off.
Write
All the grinlings run off.
They tell the slinx that something
called a _ _ _ _ _ _ _ _ is coming.

At last, the slinx dashes across to the big pot and jumps in.

If he pushes the lid up a little bit, he can see what is going on.

Then a big, metal boot
comes stamping down, just missing the pot.

The slinx grips the rim of the pot.

He can see that the Honkbonk is very, very big.

In fact, he is colossal!

What is he going to do?

Will he catch him?

The slinx ducks down.

Draw the slinx in the pot and the boot crashing down.

Write

Will the Honkbonk _ _ _ _ _
the slinx?

This is the Honkbonk.

He is a metal man.

His legs are as thick as tree trunks.

There are six green buttons on
his chest.

There is a big metal basket on
his back.

He has big crab-hands.

If he steps on the pot he will crush
it flat.

Draw the Honkbonk.

Write

This is the _____.

He is a _____ man.

The Honkbonk stomps across to one of the plastic and glass houses.

HONK! HONK! HONK!

It is astonishing.

He just picks up the house and grabs a handful of grinlings.

HONK! HONK! HONK!

Nothing can stop him.

Draw the Honkbonk grabbing the grinlings.

Write

The Honkbonk _ _ _ _ _ up one of the houses and catches some of the grinlings.

The grinlings are yelling and struggling, but the Honkbonk does not intend to let them go.

He drops them into the metal basket on his back, and snaps down the lid.

Then off he stomps, honking with happiness.

HONK! HONK! HONK!

The Honkbonk cannot stand the grinlings.

He just loves to catch them.

Write
The Honkbonk flings the grinlings into his metal _ _ _ _ _ _ .
Then he _ _ _ _ _ _ off.

The slinx creeps out of the
big pot.

He is dripping wet.

He picks up a blanket and rubs off
the mess.

The rest of the grinlings come out
of the houses.

They are very upset.

The slinx asks them what will
happen to the grinlings in the
Honkbonk's basket.

They tell him that the Honkbonk
will lock the grinlings up in his big
metal prison.

Draw the slinx dripping wet.
Write
The big ___ is full of
dinner.

The grinlings tell the slinx that the Honkbonk often attacks them.
Unless they can stop him, he will catch them all.
They will all end up in prison.
They tell the slinx that this prison is at the bottom of one of the cliffs.
The Honkbonk lives in a tent next to the prison.

Write
The grinlings tell the slinx that the Honkbonk lives in a ____ under the cliffs.

The slinx thinks that it is very sad.
The grinlings have fed him and
given him somewhere to sleep.
He cannot let them down.
He must help them now that they
have a problem.
He tells them that he will think of
a plan to get rid of the Honkbonk.
The grinlings are very happy.
They thank him very much.
The slinx sits down to do a bit
of thinking.

Draw the slinx sitting down.
Write
The slinx tells the grinlings that
he will _ _ _ _ them.
Now he must do
some _ _ _ _ _ _ _ _ .

1. What colour is the sun on Zaxon? (2)
2. Why is it a good job that the slinx can jump well? (4)
3. What can the slinx see at the top of one of the cliffs? (6)
4. Why does the slinx lick his lips? (8)
5. Why do the grinlings stop eating? (10)
6. What does the slinx jump into? (18)
7. What is on the Honkbonk's chest? (20)
8. Where does the Honkbonk put all the grinlings he catches? (24)
9. Why is the slinx dripping wet? (26)
10. Where does the Honkbonk live? (28)